AMSTERDAM
MIND
SCENARIO

AMSTERDAM
MIND
SCENARIO

TCOTPE

MILAN PAPIC

authorHOUSE®

AuthorHouse™ UK Ltd.
1663 Liberty Drive
Bloomington, IN 47403 USA
www.authorhouse.co.uk
Phone: 0800.197.4150

Published by AuthorHouse 09/18/2013

ISBN: 978-1-4918-7774-6 (sc)
ISBN: 978-1-4918-7712-8 (hc)
ISBN: 978-1-4918-7775-3 (e)

Hello From The Capital

It started as the only way.

That night I was really scared for my life!! Question without answer.
Just finished my joint, preparing to go, in that moment a man appeared in
front of me!!
Never saw this person before!! He brought
drinks at the table. Few words, the rest was silence.
Few minutes later, I've started to write my thoughts!!
These "thoughts" were created by advices from the people with who I've been
sharing friendship in my life.
I have started to write, what I should do to continue, what I should do to
heal myself.
In that October's night of the year 2011, in cafe "ZEN" eastern part of
Amsterdam, I've started this text.
Few days later, "Amsterdam mind scenario" was born, continued through
different people, different minds, different moments from all around the
planet Earth.

After this, you are going to Love forever.

Let me tell you something in a simple fact.

Come Back.

You need to take your time.

Tipic Point.

Atelier 688.

Where the life never ends.

We will stay forever.

Pooling Exercises.

You need to understand.

Think before.

Why to be together?

The rain is wet.

Rivers are cool.

Shower water supposed to be warm.

When the richness comes out.

There are some things that stay forever.

Time to celebrate.

Recognized reality.

Free again.

Now you know where I am.

If you listen very well, you can hear the silence coming.

Make it MORE!!

You write my mind.

We have a lot of paradise.

Kunst is behind we.

We saw it long before.

Streets-bicycles.

Water from Prinsengracht.

Everybody's missing something.

My best payed vacation.

Where the creativity is visible.

Paint the Universe.

It's open for.

Because we are the first.

It's about new you.

I've lived all of them.

I am loved.

Dress up your chair.

You are my sign!

I want to do it in the morning.

If you wanna go crazy; go crazy with me!

Take care about your wind.

The first time in the books.

The only clown in town.

Why did you leave so fast?

Is that still or again??

Always lead.

Installing ideas.

Trudi's lying.

Buddy call.

If you are everywhere, they can't MISSed you.

This is a solution for all.

Don't pose.

I am calculating the truth.

We are all in!!

Usually, I can understand everything.

Leave me your clone.

Instruments of life.

Distant lover.

Know that you are loved.

What am I doing??

From bed to bed.

Pure interest is shit!!

Book your city.

Just a lovely face.

Let's make it shine more.

Say something.

What are you going to do next 8h30min??

Just positive.

Gentleman.

Love is free.

Light line.

Can we believe in our minds??

Champagne Limousines.

When is the birthday of the place?

Every day!!

All girls stop to move.

That's exactly the way it goes.

Not for sale!!

It's all about the choice.

Better to be here, at least some times.

You are all my reasons . . . .

I'm having my date of now.

Don't jump in the past.

Create a good flow.

I didn't answer a thing.

LEADING LOVE.

We are rich with luck.

We need to discover more.

One stop.

If you can chew it, you can do it.

Get some light.

Everybody need to think.

It's good to know what you do.

Everything's happening for the first time.

Always hear them, but never listen.

I just let it go.

Sorry for open minds.

Stay close to you dream.

Molecules man!!

How many beautiful are going to happen??

Light district.

New year's always happening!!

Rest keeper.

Up jumping point.

Look at it as it is a challenger.

Born to feel good.

It's just me again.

We're always in some history.

Particularly constantly.

The mind leads in that direction.

Working with the center.

Living Art.

It's coming this way.

Be gentle.

Dot goes to the point.

We should take 2.

Everybody's sleeping.

Past is just in the story.

You need to know to give.

Everybody needs a story.

Dam square, Leidseplein, there is something I can't explain.

Is it somewhere else?

I was where it doesn't exist.

The family is alright.

Oti Amsterdam.

Are you my night tonight?

You said it, you meant it!

What I'm going to do?

Where you can't get stuck.

We always remember.

It doesn't matter where the world is.

We do with.

Are we all getting older?

Kind of the same way for every one, even if it's not.

Life as the main business.

It's up to you here.

Nobody can't lie himself.

Eye in the sky.

If you don't dream, you're sleeping.

A man and a legend.

Dream in.

Art Queen.

We've got the same, let's do it!!

Cupid strikes twice!!

Here my dear.

Past mine.

I know it, and you know it to.

Paint and peace.

It comes in waves like everything.

Recreated

Everything comes in once.

Very clean, very pure, very beautiful.

It just goes on and on.

We are already in the future.

You got it in a flight.

Magic man.

I came back from.

I think I wrote letters.

It's flying to you.

Living points.

If you choose to live, it supports you.

Let's spend them together.

What you would like?

You can do many things with it.

Kiss the Lady.

Time to choose our Kingdom.

You got to play Love.

White bear.

Do it with respect.

Buy the idea.

Time for the cloud.

Mine will come.

I think we've created a good reality.

Love stoned.

Shake your money maker.

There's always somebody.

Reality is better than a dream.

It's not only what you see in the mirror.

Temporary insanity.

Kingdom without crown.

Country without army.

Richness without money.

Wisdom without school.

Constant connection with heavens.

Identity without body.

Death without regrets.

Suck the blanket.

They don't understand the difference.

Flat scream!!

Time traveler.

I've lived them all.

This is the way you feel.

Let's call it some how.

Don't wonder.

Sun stones.

We are one liner.

Road to peace.

You are the most beautiful.

For you, I am.

History is the future.

You are loved.

I know enough.

9 lines.

Light the candles, let them come.

You can be rich on many different…

Beautiful us.

This is not a story about one man.

This is not a story about one company.

This is the story about one world.

Light's starting man.

We are Universal.

We believe in the same dream.

You go some where, you're still here.

The coolest Galaxy ever!!

I want tomorrow!!

Tales of power.

Frogs on steroids.

Two days of walk.

Two years too young.

Everybody's missing everything.

I feel like I have time.

Liz my face.

Don't poke the liver.

Youngsters.

We are not samurais.

Don't buy, if they don't have what you need.

These are the real informations.

We can see far enough.

We have to go up.

This is for now.

You need to imagine first.

Sailors believe in gold.

1889.

This don't belong to US.

Everybody's saying it.

This is the life road.

How many Minos we are??

If you know the first, you know everything.

The knowledge never dies.

Read the paintings.

We deserve each other.

There is too much standing alone.

Emotions leading us.

We can generate so much Love.

Consciousness is the most important.

Details are the difference between success and failure.

Take off the price.

Busy work.

Discover your world.

All we need is food.

Are you crazy or something?

Find your place.

Just a smile away!!

Fly to the light.

Languages may differ, but the message remains the same.

It's a new regular.

Do it every where you can.

Paradise for real.

Naturally arranged.

Don't talk in between.

It's a gallery/ bar/ lounge.

Positive feedback.

Member forever.

Set me on the high light.

Be your own Sun.

Aura pang pang protection.

Feeling style.

Back to paradise.

It can only be better.

This crowd grows!!

Be living in Angels.

Sun worship.

The winner never quits.

Life time guaranty.

The city who loves you.

Happy non endings.

It belongs with you.

It will always be beautiful.

No need to prove it!!

It's not finished.

Continue.

Lovely sounds.

Everything moves.

Be real.

Let's do it now.

One, than all.

Take the understanding.

Top of the part . . . !!

We don't have any problems, to be honest.

Full creation!

Donations yeah!!

Wings grows again.

Night destiny.

ORGANic farm.

Beautiful, highly educated, rich and horny.

Give me a minute!!

One more time we need to stop the time.

Fresh new.

Don't compare new with old and bad.

Preventive!!!

If you don't know both, you'll not know what to choose.

It's just so close to your capacities.

Time is designed.

Every day, you can discover the golden mine.

It's coming, it's coming!!

Everybody's inn!!

Revitalization.

All I have is in my mind.

I need some yellow.

I am known for my words!!

Parallel worlds.

The center of good life.

Mr. Idea.

Powerepuptalks.

SOULed out!!

We are alive!!

The whole configuration.

We were here before.

They've been sailing far.

A lot's of signs.

The essence of color?

Planetary tastings.

Everything included!!

Amsterdam's way.

Golden open hand.

Sky land.

It's not easy to leave the paradise.

Future will prove it.

Now you are original.

Consent about paradise.

Painting

The world of silence

The world of loneliness

So close

So far

If it could moves

And touch you now

When it looks alive

Painting of beauty

Might stay forever

Wisdom could became

Visible.

As good visible is.

If you don't move, the world stops.

You have to practice.

The Stars.

Focus on one but not in one sense.

Can we create the Sun?

See your next step.

All that is because of this.

Be wise to choose.

Where the whole city is your neighborhood.

It's time to realize dreams.

For the moment, nobody knows.

How many reasons could be found?

Say it when it's ready.

More than everything for every thing.

Location is not located.

Don't let your mind be scared by something new.

Keeping your mind open, keeps your life open.

Let's go little further.

All believes in one.

Unwritten rules.

Smiling memories.

The way I choose.

I've never read about dignity.

You need to write it down.

It's good, that's all!!

Not like they want to.

Does it lead over there?

Streets & bars.

And than you know and than you see.

Super baby.

Meet yourself.

True can be different.

To our beauty.

Viva!!

You don't know how lucky you are.

People live for one thing.

Don't ask nothing.

Sleep when you can!

Play as you say.

The choice is all we got.

There is one interesting thing about all.

I love you my Queen.

They don't know nothing about it.

Level club!!

Everything coming out, coming from here.

Keep it for you.

The feeling of silence.

I saw a woman loving a man.

I know the way now.

Zero is some thing!!

NY is coming back home.

Depends how you put yourself on there.

I'm so Zendout.

Another day in the Capital . . .

Where the secrets are.

Very nine.

I can feel the colors.

Recover and go again.

Respect is enough.

For the Love.

Young spirits.

Always ready to go.

Make sure that you see as it is.

Keep your vision going!!

Is it somewhere closer?

Tram walking.

I know, but it's my life now.

Luckily, I never had it.

I lost it everywhere I was.

Surprises on the road.

What's more, what's left?

It's hard to think about something else in that moment.

You need it for the rest of tomorrow.

Make the cake.

Where's the camera??!!

The first pleasure of life??

Who is the Captain?

Who is the Governor??

Who is the Ministre??

Who is the President??

Who is the King??

Who is, who is??.

We all need Sun!!

Maps, maps, maps.

Just simple.

The way back is always different.

What ever the time is.

If you know, it's enough.

You wanna maths delivery.

You have to win them all.

Higher reality.

I'm starting it for the rest of the time.

If it's not changed today, it will not change tomorrow.

All pictures.

Alive water.

She thinks school, I think is cool.

All we know, coming from the past.

Bicylicking.

We just painted over.

Just smile.

We'll see how you feel, we'll see how you make me feel.

Because they're laying down.

Give it to me, take it from me.

The sound in again.

We're good now.

Satisfaction.

After a little while, we all come together.

Not important.

Time needs to be in a ser w ice.

Let's get normal some how.

Today is my day of landing.

From one we went to two, so easy.

Then to 3.

Then?!

The future belongs to him who believes in his dreams.

Leaders do not create products, but the meaning and sense.

Being awkward to the world, is following your dreams!!

Direct call.

I'm missing it every time I don't have it.

Good coffee is tremendous!!

Friday is Wednesday.

Every road leads somewhere.

Starts from now.

It's about how you C. O. P. E. with it.

Ideas are not dying.

Shiny, open, wide.

Famous, famous, famous.

To the light, than on the left.

We are the wave of freedom!!

Believe to your reality.

No tricks in disguise.

I'll do my best.

If you want to go, you can still go.

Life, we make it.

Where I should continue?

Every body should be able to upgrade.

I want to be more in it.

I'll bell!

I am non ending story.

Blog inn ovations.

What you would like to hear??

Every zip is different.

It is magical.

Let it go!!

Are you genius??

Solid shaver.

Don't brake the wave!!

Tie shaper.

Instant high!!

That's the way . . . . ! !

We know more when we wake up.

House dealer.

Bridge traffic.

Do we still talk about same things?

Where do WE go?

He says something,

I say something.

The weather is good, everything is getting better!!

We need to.

You can never know.

That's the only reason why they are leaving.

Find a connection.

Don't let them think you.

Show it any time you can.

You can do something about everything.

Don't let them take a piece of you!!

Laguna of power.

With you, this world is different.

I'm painting you with Love!!

Creativity of Glory.

Than, just a happiness.

I see different destinations.

Without shoes.

View without end.

It have to continue.

Happiness is our creation.

We are every thing.

It is happening in a right moment.

Let's go there again.

Magic getting bigger.

More you let, more you get!!

Make the turn of your mind.

It's alright, now I know a bit about tomorrow.

They did it before.

Sunny tropical Island.

Here it is.

Thx to the Rain and the Sun.

They are back.

There is no only one beginning.

How do we look to the world?

One home.

Awakening, you have to enjoy!!!!!!!!!

Message always goes further.

I need to see my mind.

Life having time.

Everybody's using somebody!!

I know all ways.

How memory works??

I need a transport to swim.

Do it by the main entrance!!

To all crazy free people!!

Don't tell me, show me!!

When the Sun is coming from inside.

Are we crazy or what?!

He's going into the sound.

Nice enjewision.

It's all within.

Pacha mama.

De friends.

On the beach.

You don't expect what's next.

Everybody needs to get activated.

Than we start to talk to the people.

It belongs to everybody.

Just a moment please.

Do we pull or push?

Do you also want 2?

Inspiration is coming.

People are obliged to wear it.

Using reality.

Some how, new vision.

Surprising arrivals.

Destiny is where infinity ends.

Royal night design.

It's about, it's all about it.

Drink your beer, smoke your joint and never forget!

Evolution of existence.

Let it rest.

Sounds of the moment.

It is what it is, not more or less.

Just accept it.

We sell money, we can sell any thing, everything.

The names.

What color is the sacred.

Where everything begins.

Is it ours?

Turn off the TV, turn on your mind.

Keepers of the peace.

You can't hide me, you can't steal me, you need to share me.

Upgrade the glasses.

Saturday never ends.

We all go there.

We all go there.

It's coming through the minds.

Sandwich pret.

It rains but it stays.

That's the life gate.

Time is still here.

I'm giving something back.

Sailing the night.

It's all about choice.

Follow the stars!!

It keeps you young.

But I can fix my way out.

There's a lot of knowledge.

Everybody is.

All feelings every day.

Life is set up on that way.

The night is getting warmer.

We all need to remember.

Keep from going crazy, and listen to the rain.

Strawberry skin.

Rise and shine.

AGAIN!!

You know where the diamonds are.

I like botox more than chicken.

NO, is not an answer.

Energy is one.

No rain till Brooklyn.

Painted by his own hand.

The Code!

Scan it!

It's a winsdor.

Today, I'm going through my mind.

Is this hospitality?

If we like each other, we like each other.

It's my mistake.

See the languages.

Traces.

All they said.

There's no plan.

Black wine, red bottles.

It takes time.

It's a long ride.

Then you have a fog, rain, then you have the Sun.

Slow down.

Be different.

Keep on trying.

We are creating this World.

Rethink.

Connections.

Experience.

Share!!

These moments are worth much more.

God speed.

Got to be good for everybody.

We go only for one.

There's nothing bad.

Time is relative.

Live the moment.

More you have them good, more your life is good.

Forget enough.

Take it easy9.

ART & Party.

A day without bubbles, has not been lived.

What is happening here?!

Those changes.

How many times you don't know who you are??

Why does it happening??

I love you brother, I like your style!!

How we're cracked Doctor??!!

It's just a third day.

Love is still here!!

She left.

Hope, believe, means . . .

When you know that is the real one!!

Can't touch it.

Open eyes can't see.

Till you can feel.

I don't think that way.

Galaxy is here!!

You are never alone.

We don't have any questions.

We have only answers.

Everything you see is Artofficial.

When you feel at home everywhere.

There's always something happening.

I'm losing my point of now.

But the other will be here.

Right now!!

It's about who you are already.

Gold mines all around.

Show of the colors.

Real people.

Hidden beauties.

Time to believe that we exist.

Music keeps together.

Lead your future.

Wisdom.

Is in you.

New life.

We always knew it!!!!!!!!

Crazy, beautiful and very nice.

Always when I come back.

Watching him getting empty and full!

Life is Love.

Time will never come before.

Never been better.

That's why beauty exists.

See things coming.

Friendship never stops.

ZLZRBISJ.

Explore the flow.

It's everywhere where you are.

We did it in the painting.

I sleep easy bro.

Work it out!!

Don't let nothing stop you!

Always be yourself!

Never think bad!

Life teaches!

Every thing is going to be perfect!

You get what you can take!

All believes in one.

Unwritten rules.

Smiling memories!

The way I choose!

What you do, comes back to you!

Only thing you can do, is to be happy!

This is how it should be!

The city is packed!!

The best quality, the best price!!

We got to do it again!!

Within.

Don't kiss the Queen!!

Can't see the future that far.

Now we are in a different thing, with the same knowledge.

Where is the beginning of ending?

Inside story.

It was what it was, now it is what it is!!

They have imagination under control.

If they don't come between us, they don't exist.

It's coming back again.

I still can believe to myself.

I don't do nobody.

Today is good.

Do we live the past?

I didn't see any around.

Let's motivate the world to talk.

We all coming from some where.

We were also creating the history.

A little hack.

We are in the same time.

Knowledge is inside.

Full screen button.

One is enough.

Everybody need to think about it.

You are ambassador.

You are ambassador.

Before you left, I was already there.

You are the Architect of my dreams.

You are real.

Now you're going to Love forever.

Next time I pay.

Just see it.

You know, it's just if you want.

It's OK, I know you.

Just can't wait to see you again.

Don't Google on me.

Keep them all!

Here we go.

The style of now.

Just ask and you get it.

Right now, I feel so good.

Do it with Love.

No step, no freedom.

Just use it again.

Give it a different name.

Make something out of what you have.

My lover is black.

Always look at the clean side of the mirror.

Winners spirit.

We have to plant the trees.

Take care about beauty.

Don't use love!

Which color do you see around me?

We have a different vision!!

Open the last button.

I can't land!!!??

Air traces.

Love is the only solution.

It works for real.

Next table story.

Maybe they're busy cloning the planet.

Let's make some.

It's a pinK code honey.

Organic was my nex.

We are more free!!

The whole World every day!!

Openings.

Here we are again.

Every body's going to die, but let's have some fun first!!

Send your mind to another destination.

Real artists.

So white night.

This is not completely real.

Celebrating incredible.

Sussie's therapy.

One of the brothers.

Never forget what we're saying!!!!!!!!!!!!!!!!!!

What's that big?

I see a lot of Zeppelins coming!!

Body count.

I don't remember the story.

Any way, I've missed Alpee.

Cash bags!!

They left further, it was too cool.

We all have common dreams.

Need to stay the same.

Love him!!

He loves you!!

I've got the time more than anyone else in this world.

Success is a journey, not a destination.

The mind of this time.

Everybody's welcome.

I see, all is coming to us.

Life as the main business.

I want to use your qualities.

Miss Earth & Mister Life.

One day in a time.

Just a second and it goes like what.

189 Nations.

Different colors.

Different cultures.

Different religions.

Same way of thinking!!

State of mind.

Always possible!

I'll be your memory.

Everything is everywhere.

We are objective.

Leave the space open.

Punch your party.

We're doing exactly the same things!!

It's not important where I'm from, if you know where I travel.

Rolling stoned.

Double the bubble.

Brand your mind.

Time for the sound.

Keep attention on the last thing.

The Sun is shining now.

Just like there.

Art looks real.

Still on the party.

Need a time to refresh.

1.000.000's thanks to the Angels.

The world is late.

Use the past.

Don't forget the lessons.

Be the rhythm.

Feel like before.

Respect.

Trust.

Friendship.

We know all about happening.

Little bit less than perfect.

It's not about the money.

Do you need a calculator??

Time lap.

It doesn't exist, but it's already there.

Too no lyrics.

The worst things ever happened, happened to the greatest.

Everything is for the time being:

Future comes through the vision.

Leave the time follow you.

Life is a journey.

Live the life you love, love the life you live.

General's point of view.

Go for your vision.

The sounds of the water.

Tiger's colors.

Are you Buddhist?

But I am also Muslim and Catholic.

All in one point.

Use your Art.

Everybody needs water.

Do not hate.

We all need to drink it!!

Yes we do!!

Where we are now?

Your reality is here, right now!!

In the same breath.

We make US one.

This is an official society voice. LOL.

Take care about my peace as it's yours.

I know how waves work.

Different times for different views.

You're my poem.

Box-option.

Everything is already accepted.

The World is 1 now!!

I know when to be smart.

We make the World 1!!

We have more.

To the freedom.

It's a good chapter.

When you do what you want to do.

Space design.

I am the leader, you're my guide.

Very important indeed.

It's just K.

That lovely body needs waves.

On the top of the roof!!

From all around the around.

Artistic love name.

I'm not.

You are already.

100% International!!!

I got my wings back!!

Keep your beach clean.

Can we organize more festivals??

Gold Generators.

Get your informations from the taste.

Listen to what you think.

I believe.

You just need to feel good.

Look at your life now.

Story starts later.

IF YOU CAN, RECOGNIZE THESE!!

Don't make mistakes in a smoking area.

We need to relax.

Life goes over it.

This was over over!!

The place to be.

I don't talk like a political, but I have.

Nice blue eyes.

It's just a game for one man.

Day by day.

One is not enough.

We're just going.

You're lucky to go.

Where the life is real.

How long??

Still goes on.

Because we are children.

If I can't see it, it can't see me.

Always been there, but not before.

Good goes into the good.

Let's go, let's go crazy!!

Where are the stars??

Here they are!!

High as the light!!

Week, week, week, weeks.

Colors of the light.

Where everything continues.

Feel good, drink Champagne.

Just be, whatever.

Never give up.

Healthy, Happy, Powerful, Rich.

Future is now.

Live this moment, this moment is your life.

Eternity is possible!!

Do not kill, LOVE,

The city of Life

AMSTERDAM

The Capital of the Planet Earth

Special thanks to: Mr. Rousetos, Old Good Man, Vasilije Spirta,

Robert Nesta Bob Marley, Oti Amsterdam, Danny Amsterdam,

Zarko Almuli, Wild Bil Amsterdam, Uncle John London,

Corrina Agios Nikolaos, Momcilo Papic, Vojin Malencic,

Jean Agios Nikolaos, Paolo Nassif, Thomas Koenen, Joey Maldonado,

Naleye Sultan Buddista the 1st, Dr. Stasey Smith, Yolanda Schonberger,

Mick Agios, Onno Klein, Linda Amsterdam, Bass Brumans, Brigget George,

SS, JJ, Anthony Martinez, Guido Paludanus, Dimitris Mavroforos,

Ismael Zeirouh, Donald Schaffer, Raphael Espana, Abdel Aziz, Javaid Malik,

Anita Vega, Erwin Blaas, Loef my neighbor, Mike Zaitsoff, Ernst, WAM,

Rastafarai Amsterdam, Manolis Pangalos, Job Reuten, Mark Peeters,

Dez Vylenz, Stan de Kanter, Hisham Benyahia, Johannes Scholte, Riblja Corba,

Soner Oncel, Mladen Cumbo, Sonja Koops, Joris Jan Reuten,

Tatiana Aphroditsiac, Cem Guden, Abdelilah Hyati, Manuel Guerrero,

Yannick Sinclair Noomen, Mike Van Wetten, Boris Viskovic, Darius Amsterdam,

Michael Nunes, Berislav Viskovic, Rose Bertins, Collin Linnekamp,

Mohamed Bouali, Christophe Rauch, Denny Amsterdam, Sasha Nikitin,

Philipp Roth, Elizabeth Bruin, MARIA, Makkie Van Heuvel, Alejandro de la Tore,

Victoria d'Amsterdam, Tara, Greek Voyager, Arnold Amsterdam,

Reko Amsterdam, Mirtxe, Miss Laura, Reiky De Valk, Milano easy9.

ZEN

Milan Papic, came on the Planet Earth the sixth of June 1977 in the city of Zrenjanin. Raised in the family house in the village of Secanj, with sister Jovana, by mother Bosa and father Momcilo.

Where ever you go, what ever you do, don't forget respect, friendship, happiness, love, yourself..